WWW.ZODIACSERVICES.NET

Presents

MBA BASICS IN 24 HOURS!

A SIMPLE HANDBOOK OF SERVICE MARKETING Q & A

ADDITIONAL BOOK 4 – SERVICE MARKETING AND DISCUSSION QUESTIONS

Life Grows With Us!

SIMPLE & EASY WAY TO UNDERSTAND THE BASICS OF BUSINESS ADMINISTRATION TOPICS EASILY IN SUMMARY AND KEYWORDS WITH 8 EFFECTIVE CHAPTERS & ADDITIONAL TOPICS!

By

G.R. Narasimhan

Welcome to Zodiac Services MBA chapters in brief with eight effective and additional special topics given as individual books!

GOOD LUCK TO BE A BUSINESS ADMINISTRATOR!

Copyright © 2020 by **Narasimhan Ranganathan @ G. R. Narasimhan**

All rights reserved. No part of this book/e-book may be reproduced, distributed or transmitted in any form or by any means, including photocopying, recording or other electronic or mechanical methods, without the prior written permission of the author, except in the case of brief quotations embodied in critical reviews and certain other non-commercial uses permitted by copyright law. For permission requests, write to the author, addressed 'Attention: Author', at the address below.

Zodiac Services, Chennai, India

Get more contact details and numbers from:

www.zodiacservices.net [or] mail to info@zodiacservices.net

Ordering Information for hardcopies:

Quantity sales – Special discounts are available on quantity purchases by corporations, associations and others. For details, contact the author at the address above.

NOV 2020 – First Edition

Released and Published in India

****
Legal Disclaimer/ Notice

All the chapters, topics, discussions, statements, e-books/books and web contents including this MBA in 24 hours either online or offline are under business administration category. This guide is recommended to get simple understanding and guidance of bachelors or masters in business administration only. Readers are requested to apply their own knowledge or refer or consult their own tutors or masters before acting on any of the recommendations for examinations and related activities. Neither Zodiac services nor any of its promoters, members or author (if anyone) holds any responsibility of any losses/ liability incurred (if any/ if you end up in loss) by acting on the same as given to follow in presentations or examinations. We or Zodiac services, Chennai/head or branch offices anywhere in the world, are not responsible for, and will not compensate in any way for, any loss or damage related directly or indirectly from/to the information on this book/e-book. Thanks for your cooperation!

****

ABOUT THE AUTHOR

G.R. Narasimhan – Sr. Consultant for technology and business under **RNP - Zodiac Services Chennai** which serves the people in abroad study, alternative beliefs/therapies like astrological predictions, prayers, remedies, prasanam (divine words) and vedic guidance for short- or long-term problems, vaastu, numerology, gem stones, yantras, mantras or rituals (related areas), yoga, meditation, counselling and alternative therapies consulting. Business & education, soft skills/software/electronics & communication training & promotion, web designing, career counselling and Internet & social media marketing are additionally served. Assisting the entrepreneurship business for the above mentioned areas to serve better for the clients, **G.R. Narasimhan** also the author of few e-books called 'A Simple guide to Vedic Astrology', 'Inverted Universal Meditation & Engineering/production', 'Secrets of Equity Stocks to make Millions', 'Symbolic Meditation & Developing ESP' and many other (are already available in Amazon) having extended experience in IT + Management areas developed website and online marketing using different business strategies and continue the service very well to extend further including this 'MBA Basics in 24 Hours with Additional Topics – Service Marketing and Questions & Answers' –specifically based on the business administration topics applied overall in the academic curriculum. With the continuous extraordinary ability and skills in research/study and experience, he is able to explain and train/assist others with extended support and guidance by counselling/consulting effectively.

Great thanks and good luck for everyone reading this book on 'MBA Basics in 24 Hours' with almost all the areas of basic business administration or career growth individually or as a group. For any queries and feedback, you can contact directly via email to info@zodiacservices.net, info@astroservices.in or astronara@gmail.com.

CONTENTS

Topics	Page Numbers
INTRODUCTION	5
CHAPTER 1 - MARKETING OF SERVICES	7
CHAPTER 2 - FUNDAMENTAL DIFFERENCES BETWEEN GOODS AND SERVICES	9
CHAPTER 3 - AN OVERVIEW OF THE SERVICE SECTOR	13
CHAPTER 4 - THE CONSUMER DECISION PROCESS IN SERVICES MARKETING	16
CHAPTER 5 - ETHICAL ISSUES IN SERVICE MARKETING	19
CHAPTER 6 - DEFINING AND MEASURING CUSTOMER SATISFACTION	22
CHAPTER 7 - DEFINING AND MEASURING SERVICE QUALITY	25
CHAPTER 8 - SERVICE FAILURES AND RECOVERY STRATEGIES	29
CHAPTER 9 - CUSTOMER RETENTION	32
CHAPTER 10 - PUTTING TOGETHER: CREATING THE SEAMLESS SERVICE FIRM	34
CHAPTER 11 - SERVICE DELIVERY PROCESS	37
CHAPTER 12 - THE PRICING OF SERVICES	41
CHAPTER 13 - DEVELOPING THE SERVICE COMMUNICATION MIX	44
CHAPTER 14 - MANAGING THE FIRMS PHYSICAL EVIDENCE	47
CHAPTER 15 - PEOPLE ISSUES MANAGING SERVICE EMPLOYEES/STAFFS	52
CHAPTER 16 - PEOPLE ISSUES MANAGING SERVICE CONSUMERS	55
CONCLUSION	58

INTRODUCTION

Business Administration is the combination of different areas of skills in management. Managing and maintaining several departments or areas of activities described in a single umbrella or vertical called management of business administration. The following areas are the main topics or chapters for the discussion under business administration, mostly common for any bachelors or master's studies.

- Principles & Practices of Management
- Human Resource Management
- Financial Management
- Marketing Management
- Organisational Behaviour
- Managerial Economics
- Strategic Management
- Management Information Systems

Then there are several branches extended in business administration like foreign trade, global marketing, international business, social work, information technology, finance, human resources etc. These above eight topics considered to summarise and define important brief summary and keywords under which various chapters for each topic are given (published in Amazon).

This book covers the summaries and definitions of keywords for the topic 'Service Marketing and Q & A discussions' with the following chapters.

MARKETING OF SERVICES, FUNDAMENTAL DIFFERENCES BETWEEN GOODS AND SERVICES, AN OVERVIEW OF THE SERVICE SECTOR, THE CONSUMER DECISION PROCESS IN SERVICES MARKETING, ETHICAL ISSUES IN SERVICE MARKETING, DEFINING AND MEASURING CUSTOMER SATISFACTION, DEFINING AND MEASURING SERVICE QUALITY, SERVICE FAILURES AND RECOVERY STRATEGIES, CUSTOMER RETENTION, PUTTING TOGETHER: CREATING THE SEAMLESS SERVICE FIRM, SERVICE DELIVERY PROCESS, THE PRICING OF SERVICES, DEVELOPING THE SERVICE COMMUNICATION MIX, MANAGING THE FIRMS PHYSICAL EVIDENCE, PEOPLE ISSUES MANAGING SERVICE EMPLOYEES/STAFFS & PEOPLE ISSUES MANAGING SERVICE CONSUMERS

Some of the chapters given with examples of Indian economy/trading/service-related terms. But readers must understand the concepts of their own country's business & economy and other areas. Most of the answers are gathered from varies online/ offline resources and in turn makes life easier for the people to prepare for any exams or case studies.

As it has high level of contents in brief which can be covered in three hours maximum, readers can read other books from different authors to gain in-depth knowledge of the given business management and administration. This book gives quick glance & easy go chapters for any situation like interview, short answering and overall explanation to present others. Good Luck!

CHAPTER 1 - MARKETING OF SERVICES

DISCUSSION QUESTIONS

1. Define the following terms: goods, services, and products.

Ans- **Goods**
Adam Smith (1776) stated that goods have exchangeable/negotiable value and so a characteristic of a good is that its ownership rights can be established and exchanged.

Services
Services are the non-physical, intangible parts of our economy, as opposed to goods, which we can touch or handle. Services, such as banking, education, medical treatment, and transportation make up the majority of the economies of the rich nations. They also represent most of the emerging nations' economies.

Product
A product is any item or service you sell to serve a customer's need or want. This definition might seem simple, but as you will learn in this guide, there is a lot more to a product than its at-first-glance attributes and what the customer thinks they are paying for.

2. Why is it difficult to distinguish between many goods and services? Use the scale of market entities and the molecular model concept to explain your answer.

Ans-The distinction between goods and services is not always perfectly clear. In reality, most services contain some tangible components, while most goods also contain intangible components. It is difficult to say whether a pure service or a pure good even exist. The scale of market entities helps us understand whether the product under consideration is tangible-dominant or intangible-dominant.

3. Discuss the relevance of the scale of market entities to marketing myopia.

Ans-Firms that define their businesses too narrowly suffer from market myopia. Often Manufacturing/Production firms overlook the service aspects of their product offering when attempting to differentiate themselves from competitors. Similarly, service firms often neglect the tangible aspects of their product which become key indicators of consumer perceptions of quality. The scale of market entities helps us understand whether the product under consideration is tangible-dominant or intangible-dominant and recognize all aspects, both tangible and intangible, of the product offering.

4. Develop a molecular model for your College of Business.

Answers will vary, but at the core should be education (intangible) which could then be connected to academic advising (intangible), career advising (intangible), faculty and staff (tangible), building (tangible), etc.

5. Utilizing the servuction model, describe your classroom experience. How would your servuction model change as you describe the experience at a local restaurant?
Ans-Answers will vary, but at the core should be a description of the visible services cape, contact personnel/service providers, other customers/clients and invisible organization and systems.

6. Discuss the consequences of the industrial-management model.
Ans-Consequences of the industrial model affect employees/staffs and customers/clients. Employee consequences include the following: (1) Produce dead-end front-line jobs, poor pay, superficial training, no opportunity for advancement, if any, access to company benefits. (2) Has led to customer dissatisfaction, flat or declining sales revenues, high employee turnover, and little service productivity.

7. What benefits are associated with better-paid and better-trained personnel?
Ans-Companies that pay their employees/staffs more than competitors often find that as a percentage of sales, their labor costs are actually lower than industry averages. Better paid personnel tend to be more knowledgeable, more available, and more motivated to satisfy customers/clients. Similarly, the benefits of training are clear. Better trained and better-paid employees/staffs provide better service, need less supervision, and are more likely to stay on the job. In turn, their customers/clients are more satisfied, return to make purchases more often, and purchase more when they do return.

8. Discuss the relevance of the services triangle to the market-focused management model.
Ans-The service triangle depicts six key relationships that tie the firm's service strategy, the systems it operates, the firm's customers/clients, and the firm's employees/staffs together. Similarly, the market-focused management model promotes that the purpose of the firm is to serve the customer, while the purpose of how the firm is organized is to support the employees/staffs that serve the customer. The linkages that form the services triangle should flow logically from one another and support the firm's overall mission of providing superior service delivery that differentiates it from its competitors.

CHAPTER 2 - FUNDAMENTAL DIFFERENCES BETWEEN GOODS AND SERVICES

DISCUSSION QUESTIONS

1. Briefly describe how the unique service characteristics of intangibility, inseparability, heterogeneity, and perishability apply to your educational experience in your services marketing class.
Ans-They have six fundamental characteristics: **intangibility, inseparability** of production and consumption, **perishability, heterogeneity**, client-based relationships, and customer contact. **Intangibility** means that a service cannot be seen, touched, tasted, or smelled. **Heterogeneity** is variation in service quality.

2. Why is the pricing of services particularly difficult in comparison with the pricing of goods?
Ans- Pricing services is more difficult than pricing products because you can often pinpoint the **cost** of making a physical product but it's more subjective to calculate the worth of your counsel, your staff's expertise, and the value of your time.

3. What strategies has the insurance industry utilized in its attempt to minimize the effects of intangibility of the companies that have actively attempted to minimize the effects, have some companies done a better job than others? Please explain.
Ans-There is little research/study concerning insurance companies and their relationships with corporate customers/clients. Most of the previous studies have been from the insurance companies' point of view and have focused on other, although related, subjects (cf. Jaensson, 1997). Thus, there is a clear need for further research/study in this field of financial marketing with a relationship perspective. Conceptual development is needed in insurance marketing, as the financial markets are part of a dynamic business environment. One major area to be exposed is the importance of relationship management in the insurance business, particularly in terms of the relationships between insurance companies and corporate customers/clients. The aim of this report is firstly, to develop a conceptual framework from a relationship perspective for the study of insurance services' marketing, and secondly, to draw some conclusions concerning this field.

4. Discuss the implications of having the customer involved in the production process.

Ans- Manufacturing/Production companies by nature focus on engineering/production, but oftentimes they have forgotten their customers/clients/clients. A sound business case should be offering, or even co-developing, products and services that cater to customer needs. Such an outside-in perspective opens doors to new customers/clients and business possibilities, and helps align internal departments to serve customers/clients better. The trick is to encourage staff, especially engineers/techies and production staff, to engage with customers/clients constantly.

Manufacturing/Production companies, built on a strong engineering/production heritage, often overlook a key actor: the customer. Enabling staff to have more contact with customers/clients generates insights, which can be developed into services that enhance your commercial offers and build stronger customer relationship.

Too focused on production

In production-focused companies, even departments that work with customers/clients tend to get caught up in the organizational culture and struggle to bring the customer perspective into the company's operations. These companies likely focus mainly on setting up facilities and managing production and supply chain.

Misalignment between departments, from sales and marketing to production and engineering/production, impacts the products and services provided. Input from customers/clients, even when it is deemed useful, takes time to be incorporated. If companies do not understand customer needs, they are likely to incur significant costs related to preventable incidents.

Adopt an outside-in perspective

When you adopt a customer's outside-in perspective, it is easier to differentiate service issues from product and production issues. When a shipment of components is delayed, it is not only a production issue. From a customer perspective, it is mainly about a timely notice that minimizes impact on the customer's own operation. Customers/clients in general appreciate an honest discussion about your capabilities and their needs.

"If only you were able to…"

Customer complaints of course help manufacturers identify areas to be improved. However, conversations with your customers/clients, as well as their own customers/clients, often generate very useful insights and ideas of new business opportunities.

When customers/clients tell you "if only you were able to...", you are opening your world to new business possibilities. They may tell you they prefer having certain product specifications or information delivered earlier, for instance. Although your customers/clients may not know whether what they want is something you can do, such conversations are extremely valuable and productive. Customers/clients are usually willing to share their perspective, or even co-develop products and solutions with you.

A 2% increase in customer retention has the same effect as decreasing costs by 10%

Innovations empower customers/clients

Unlike product innovations, service innovations don't always require massive investment or even operational changes. Innovative services that strengthen customer relationship could be access to in-house experts and product configurators, real-time online customer support and role-based training. These services are also easy to scale up and enable more customers/clients to improve their businesses.

A sound business case

When engineers/techies and production staff interact with their customers/clients, the new insights are helpful in challenging the long-held assumptions and conventions that have kept manufacturers from focusing more on customers/clients. The resulting innovative services likely offer great value to customers/clients. Therefore, engaging with customers/clients in order to understand their business and experience is more than a good practice. It is a sound business case.

5. Discuss the reasons that centralized mass production of services is limited.

Ans-The centralized mass production of services is difficult due to inseparability. **Inseparability** is the characteristic that a service has which renders it impossible to divorce the supply or production of the service from its consumption. Other key characteristics of services include perishability, intangibility and variability.

Suggested solutions to minimize the impact of inseparability include:

- the careful selection and thorough training of public contact personnel
- manage customers/clients to enhance their service experience
- the use of multi-site locations to overcome the difficulties associated with
- centralized mass production

6. Why are standardization and quality control difficult to maintain throughout the service delivery process?

Ans- Any service delivery process goes through different workgroups to complete its tasks. This multi-group situation is true of most processes, not just service delivery. Each workgroup has its own internal needs and their own internal sub-processes. Problems arise when the needs and sub-processes of one workgroup differ from those of another workgroup. So, what is the solution: standardization/correction. By establishing and enforcing standards the service delivery process runs smoothly from workgroup to workgroup. As you might expect, the establishment of end-to-end standards can make life difficult for some workgroups (e.g. extra work), while ensuring that other workgroups benefit (by receiving useable input to their sub process). Standards usually are intended to benefit the end-to-end process but, often put extra burdens on some workgroups, while making life better for other workgroups.

CHAPTER 3 - AN OVERVIEW OF THE SERVICE SECTOR

DISCUSSION QUESTIONS

1. Rank and discuss the projected growth rates of the nine service super sectors. What do you believe is driving the growth of the three most highly ranked super sectors?

Ans- Activities within the service economy have been demonstrated by the nine service super sectors. The nine industry super sectors are financial activities, education sector, health sector, hospitality industry, professional services, transportation, wholesale and retail sector, financial activities and government sector. Service economy consist these nine super sectors of industry. Developed economy is categorized and service sector is one of them and industrial and agriculture and being other two categories (Anderson and Zeithaml 1984). Traditionally economies across the world are transitioning from agriculture to industrial economy and further service economy. Service sector ranked as first and most contributing sector in most of the economies. There is rapid increment in service sector contribution due to the information and communication technology's enabled services. Discussion on most highly ranked super sector: In 2015 it is expected that leisure and hospitality, construction and natural resources and business services are the three of nine super sectors driving the growth and lead through employment growth globally. It is because construction is growing everywhere today and people are travelling more due to the business purpose and travelling business people will obviously stay in luxurious hotels and hence hospitality business experiences the growth.

2. What is an e-service?

Ans- E-services are services which use of information and communication technologies (simply ICT). The three main components of e-services are- service provider, service receiver and the channels/networks of service delivery.

3. Service firms can learn a great deal from other firms in other industries. What strategies appear to be linked with success across the service spectrum?

Ans-Many managers/stakeholders of service businesses are aware that the strategic management (by which I mean the total process of selecting and implementing a corporate strategy) of service businesses is different from that of Manufacturing/Production businesses. This article discusses how pure service businesses are different from product-oriented businesses and why they require different strategic thinking. A pure service business is one in which the service is the primary entity that is sold.

That distinction is important because everyone in every type of business sells some element of service. In pure service businesses any transfer of a physical or concrete product is incidental to the service—for example, the written report of a management consultant. Examples of pure service businesses include airlines, banks, computer service bureaus, law firms, plumbing repair companies, motion picture theaters, and management consulting firms.

Top managers/stakeholders should ask themselves six questions about strategic management. The questions are fairly common, but the answers for service businesses are often unique.

1. Do we fully understand the specific type of service business we are in? Although service-oriented businesses are different from product-oriented businesses, the nature of the difference depends a great deal on the specific type of service business. I will present a classification scheme to help distinguish between service businesses along some important strategic dimensions.

2. How can we defend our business from competitors? Every business must consider how it can build and protect a strong competitive position. To do this, the economics of the business must be carefully analyzed. Service businesses often require different competitive strategies from those of product-oriented companies. If an enduring institution is to be created, some attention must be given to the management of economies of scale, proprietary technology, and reputation of the company.

3. How can we obtain more cost-efficient operations? Manufacturing/Production companies can improve operating leverage by, for example, purchasing faster and more reliable machinery. But most service businesses are not able to follow this approach. Other methods must be explored.

4. What is the rationale for our pricing strategy? The pricing of services is a nebulous area. Cost-based pricing is often difficult to determine, and there are few formulas for effective value-based pricing. It is important to look at pricing strategy and think about the economic and psychological effects of a change in that strategy.

5. *What process are we using to develop and test new services?* Every company depends on an ability to renew its franchise in the marketplace. The service-oriented company must pay particular attention to this area because of the difficulty of developing protectable competitive positions. The process of new-service development and testing must recognize the abstract, perishable nature of services.

6. *What acquisitions, if any, would make sense for our company?* Once the nature of the current business is understood, the acquisition question can be faced. The acquisition game in the service sector can be dangerous. More than one company has acquired a service business using only criteria that would be used in the acquisition of a product-oriented company. As several of these companies have learned, this type of analysis, although necessary, is insufficient.

4. Define and discuss the term materialismo snobbery.

Ans- Materialismo snobbery: belief that without Manufacturing/Production there will be less for people to service and so more people available to do less work. Materialismo snobbery reflects the belief that without Manufacturing/Production there will be less for people to service and more people available to do less work. As a result, the supply of labor will go up and at the same time the demand for labor will go down. Both effects will drive the price of labor down.

5. Discuss why the off shoring of services phenomenon is somewhat predictable.

Ans- Off shoring of services (OS), commonly defined as the international relocation of service activities that companies previously/earlier performed in their home country/nation, has emerged as a relevant phenomenon in international business (IB). Over the past two decades, OS has grown rapidly in the global economy and it has increasingly attracted IB scholars' attention. We systematically review the literature to map and assess the body of IB research/study focused on the OS phenomenon. To achieve our goal, we identify and analyze a total of 79 studies that appeared from 1990 to 2014 in a select group of 14 journals that are widely considered leading publishers of IB research/study. This review seeks to make a threefold contribution to the IB discipline. First, it provides an in-depth analysis of the OS literature through a synthesis of the theoretical perspectives adopted and an assessment of the empirical findings obtained. Second, it offers an organizing framework that contributes to a more nuanced understanding of the OS phenomenon. Third, it identifies emerging topics on the OS frontier and suggests potential avenues for future research/study.

CHAPTER 4 - THE CONSUMER DECISION PROCESS IN SERVICES MARKETING

DISCUSSION QUESTIONS

1. Discuss the different types of risk.
Ans- Inflation Risk
Inflation risk, sometimes called purchasing power risk, is the risk that the cash from an investment won't be worth as much in the future due to inflation changing its purchasing power. Inflation risk primarily examines how inflation (specifically when higher than expected) may jeopardize or reduce returns due to the eroding the value of the investment. In general, inflation risk is more of a concern for investors who have debt investments like bonds or other cash-heavy investments. Although inflation risk may not be the primary concern for investors, it definitely is and should be on their minds when dealing with cash flows over a long period of time in investment vehicles or when calculating expected returns. The longer cash flows are exposed, the more time inflation has to impact the actual returns of an investment and eat away at profits - specifically if inflation is at an accelerated rate.

Market Risk
Market risk is a broad term that encompasses the risk that investments or equities will decline in value due to larger economic or market changes or events.
Under the umbrella of "market risk" are several kinds of more specific market risks, including equity risk, interest rate risk and currency risk. Equity risk is experienced in every investment situation in that it is the risk an equity's share price will drop, causing a loss. In a similar vein, interest rate risk is the risk that the interest rate of bonds will increase, lowering the value of the bond itself. And currency risk (sometimes called exchange-rate risk) applies to foreign investments and the risk incurred with exchange rates for currencies - or, if the values of a certain currency like the pound goes up or down in comparison to the U.S. dollar.

Liquidity Risk
Liquidity risk is involved when assets or securities cannot be liquidated (that is, turned into cash) fast enough to ride out an especially volatile market. This kind of risk affects businesses, corporations or individuals in their ability to pay off debts without suffering losses. As a general rule, small companies or issuers tend to have a higher liquidity risk due to the fact that they may not be able to quickly cover debt obligations.

2. Regarding multiattribute models, what is the difference between the linear compensatory approach and the lexicographic approach?

Ans- **Compensatory Rule**

The compensatory rule dictates that a consumer makes decisions in terms of each relevant attribute and computes a weighted or summated score for each brand.

Lexicographic Rule

lexicographic decision rule, consumers first rank the attributes in terms of perceived importance. Then, the consumer selects the brand that performs best on the first attribute. If two or more brands tie, they are evaluated on the next most important attribute until one brand outperforms all the others (Hawkins et al., 2007). Using the same ranking as the previous rule, Mazda is the best brand option based on best price, the consumer's most important attribute.

3. Explain why consumers of services tend to be more brand loyal.

Ans- Consumers who are loyal to a brand remain customers/clients because they believe you offer a better service and higher quality than anyone else. This happens regardless of pricing or other financial reasons. This type of customer is also more likely to try out other products from the same brand.

4. Discuss the managerial implications of the client/company interface during the consumption stage.

Ans- The consumption decision process includes the pre purchase choice among alternatives, the consumer's reaction during consumption, and the post purchase evaluation of satisfaction. Here, during the consumption stage, consumers make a store choice or a non-store choice. It means deciding to purchase from a particular outlet or from catalog, Internet or variety of mail-order possibilities. The consumption of goods can be divided into three activities: buying, using and disposing. For example, the customer buys a box of detergent, uses it and disposes of the empty box after the detergent is used up.

This scenario does not apply to the consumption of service. There is no clear-cut boundary or definite sequence exists between the acquisition and the use of services because of its intangibility in nature. Due to the prolonged interactions between the customer and the service provider, the production, acquisition, and use of services become entangled and appear to be a single process. Furthermore, concept of disposal is irrelevant because of the intangibility and experiential nature of services. Service firms play an active role in customer consumption activities because services are produced and consumed simultaneously. No service can be produced or used with either the consumer or he service firm absent. Due to the extended service delivery process, many believe that the consumer's post choice assessment occurs both during and after the use of services, rather than only afterwards. Because of the above reason, this opens up the managerial accusations during the consumption of service. For example, the restaurant manager who visits dinners' tables and asks, "How is your dinner this evening"? is able to catch problems, and change the consumers perception about the services they received, which the manufacturer of a packaged good cannot. In service industry due to the company interface during the consumption process, the service provider is able to catch the problem and hence service providing company can change their way of doing business.

5. What is the difference between a role and a script?

Ans- Because of social **roles**, people tend to know what behavior is expected of them in specific, familiar settings. A **script** is a person's knowledge about the sequence of events expected in a specific setting.

CHAPTER 5 - ETHICAL ISSUES IN SERVICE MARKETING

DISCUSSION QUESTIONS

1. Discuss the difference between ethics and social responsibility

Ans- The expectations for good business ethics and corporate social responsibility are at an all-time high. Most likely, those expectations will continue to grow in the future. Since they are here to stay, it's wise to give employees/staffs a voice in what those expectations look like in practice. To ensure that your company's efforts are seen as genuine, it's important to review your expectations to ensure they dovetail with the company's mission and vision. Your involvement in such issues is something to be proud of so be certain to promote your efforts and make sure your customers/clients are aware of it. Attention to business ethics and corporate social responsibility creates a win-win situation for all stakeholders.

2. How does the public feel about the ethical behaviors of businesspeople?

Ans- According to a Business Week/Harris poll and other surveys: (1) 46% believed that the **ethical** standards of **businesspeople** were only average; (2) 90% believed that white-collar crime was somewhat or very common; (3) 76% relate the decline in **moral** standards in the United States directly to the lack of business **ethics**.

3. What are boundary-spanning personnel? What provides these employees/staffs with the opportunity to engage in ethical misconduct?

Ans- Boundary spanning gives a company the ability to grow by gaining. Boundary spanning is an important mechanism for the successful and efficient management of client-vendor relationships in Information Technology (IT) outsourcing. Vendors are often responsible for initiating boundary-spanning between the two parties, and the final effectiveness of boundary-spanning often hinges more on vendors rather than on clients. Boundary-spanners are individuals, who operate at the boundary of an organization, performing functions like external representation and information processing. The idea that boundary-spanning can become an organizational capability is well acknowledged in prior literature; but research/study regarding this process is limited. Boundary-spanning is often left to the ingenuity of the individual performing the role, preventing its development as an organizational capability. Therefore, this study attempts to uncover the process and develop the building blocks of the organizational capability in managing client-vendor relationships in IT outsourcing. We adopt an exploratory case study method for theory building to address the question, *"How do vendor boundary-spanners influence client-vendor relationships in*

IT outsourcing engagements?" We use multiple-case design (9 cases) for literal replication. Our propositions show that the practices of an effective boundary-spanner involve establishing a dyadic tie with the client-manager; strengthening the established tie based on shared context; using it to identify a joint problem; and developing interpersonal trust while solving this joint problem. The outcome of this interpersonal trust then gets appropriated through client-manager's structural networks and contributes to the vendor organization's business growth. This study uses the social capital lens to develop propositions regarding how boundary-spanners operate.

4. Which moral philosophies best describe your own personal ethical behavior? Explain

Ans- Personal ethics are moral guidelines that can help you through tough situations and make the best decisions. You are likely to use your personal ethics to develop your career and handle many different workplace scenarios. You can develop a clear and effective personal ethics statement that outlines the values you practice in professional settings.

Personal ethics is the code of ethical guidelines that guide you in your personal and professional life. They often develop from your core values and work ethic into actionable goals used in a variety of challenging situations. Your personal ethics can, and likely will, contain common ethical guidelines that other people share, but they will vary in their level of importance and how to maintain them.

Some common personal ethics include:

- Integrity
- Selflessness
- Honesty
- Loyalty
- Equality and fairness
- Empathy and respect
- Self-respect

5. Discuss the difference between an egoist and a utilitarianist.

Ans- The major difference between utilitarianism and ethical egoism is where those acts are directed. Utilitarianism focuses on the idea of the greater good. In egoism, the individual has a greater value than others, thus it is ethical to act in one's own self-interest even if it may potentially harm others.

CHAPTER 6 - DEFINING AND MEASURING CUSTOMER SATISFACTION

REVIEW QUESTIONS

1. What is meant by the description that most satisfaction scores are negatively skewed? Why does this score distribution occur?

Ans- A distribution is negatively skewed, or skewed to the left, if the scores fall toward the higher side of the scale and there are very few low scores. In negatively skewed distributions, the mean is usually less than the median, which is always less than the mode.

2. Discuss how the form of a question may influence satisfaction scores.

Ans- Generally, CSAT is used to measure how a customer feels about an interaction, product or service. For example, when a customer purchased a newly released product and you want to learn how satisfied they are with it. Using the CSAT survey, you can determine the level of their satisfaction with your newly released item. CSAT usually asks straightforward questions in order to immediately evaluate a customer's specific experience. The higher the score is, the more satisfied the customer feels with the service.

3. Discuss the relationship between customer satisfaction and customer retention.

Ans- Customer satisfaction is ensuring a customer's needs are met, his problems are handled, and he's satisfied with his experience with the company and the company's products or services. Customer retention is getting a customer to return after her first purchase and continue returning on a regular basis.

4. What are the drawbacks of listening to customers/clients and assessing customer satisfaction?

Ans- Disadvantages of Customer Satisfaction
- **Too many surveys, so little time:** Your customers/clients are bombarded with online surveys. Surveys may be simple to complete, however, some people simply don't like to complete them. Sending surveys too often can irritate customers/clients and lead to customer burnout. Customer burnout can result in low response rates or result in lower satisfaction scores, despite your reputation for providing excellent products or services.
- **Privacy Issues:** We live in a high-tech environment filled with daily doses of unwanted junk email, email solicitations, and sales calls. When taking an online survey or a phone survey (or any type of survey), it is hard for your customers/clients to believe that they aren't being tracked. Because of insecurities of releasing private information, customers/clients today are hesitant in giving out information that may lead to more junk email and unwanted calls. Make certain to assure customers/clients that the information they provide in response to your customer satisfaction surveys will not be used. Without this disclaimer, it may be difficult to receive a good response rate.

5. Define and explain the relevance of the terms predicted service, desired service, and adequate service as they pertain to customer satisfaction and service quality.

Ans-Desired service move upward incrementally due to accumulated experiences. Desired service as compared to adequate level of service is relatively stable.

Adequate service level expectation moves up and down and in response to competition& other factors.

6. What are the factors that influence customer expectations?

Ans-Factors that influence customer expectations

1. Customers/clients' needs and preferences
As a general rule, customers/clients expect brands to be able to help them at all times. In return for their continuous support, they want fast issue resolution and hassle-free transactions. Preferences like these can greatly affect customers/clients' expectations of your company. Even purchasing habits can significantly influence people's expectations. For instance, millennial consumers, who are always connected to the Internet, may prefer online shopping and online payment. Thus, you should consider all these when creating and launching your business strategies.

2. Culture or location
Buyers' expectations vary greatly across cultures and locations. In some countries, customers/clients don't want overly friendly or cheery customer service reps. Some

customers/clients, however, don't want to talk to agents that sound too businesslike or stiff. When interacting with a diverse clientele, consider their rules of etiquette and attitudes toward businesses, especially new market players. Other aspects such as timeliness and communication style should also be taken into account.

3. Experience with other companies

When managing customer expectations, consider your competition. What are your competitors doing to make customers/clients happy? Can you match or exceed their performance? What are the unique ways by which you can impress your customers/clients?

People's experience with other brands, especially with your competitors, can shape their expectations from you. They might model their preferences based on what other brands can do for them. If you can't outshine your competitors, you can't win customers/clients over.

4. Other customers/clients' feedback

These days, your customers/clients can spread the word about your brand instantly via the web. They can post their feedback on review websites and on social media, which can greatly influence your brand's image and reputation. What people say about you can change or contribute to customers/clients' perceptions of your brand. Thus, apart from ensuring consistent, high-quality performance, you should also take your online reputation management seriously. Doing so will help you build a positive identity.

CHAPTER 7 - DEFINING AND MEASURING SERVICE QUALITY

DISCUSSION QUESTIONS

1. What are the basic differences between customer satisfaction and service quality?

Ans-

The concept	Service quality	Customer Satisfaction
Judgment time	at a specific point in time	Both process and end state assessment
Perception	Evaluate the service provided	emotional and cognitive elements
Reflect Presence	evaluation (i.e., appraisal no require involvement, Refer to other experience and Promotions	emotional reaction requires. It is experiential. Need interaction.
Influence someone's behavioral intentions	Less influence	more influential

2. Discuss the basics of the SERVQUAL measurement instrument.

Ans- SERVQUAL is a multidimensional research/study instrument, designed to measure service quality by capturing respondents' expectations and perceptions along the five dimensions of service quality. The questionnaire consists of matched pairs of items; 22 expectation items and 22 perceptions items, organized into five dimensions which are believed to align with the consumer's mental map of service quality dimensions. Both the expectations component and the perceptions component of the questionnaire consist a total of 22 items, comprising 4 items to capture tangibles, 5 items to capture reliability, 4 items for responsiveness, 4 items for assurance and 5 items to capture empathy. The questionnaire is designed to be administered in a face-to-face interview and requires a moderate to large size sample for statistical reliability. In practice, it is customary to add additional items such as the respondent's demographics, prior experience with the brand or category and behavioral intentions (intention to revisit/ repurchase, loyalty intentions and propensity to give word-of-mouth referrals). Thus, the final questionnaire may consist of 60+ items and typically takes at least one hour, per respondent, to administer. The length of the questionnaire combined with sample size requirements contribute to substantial costs in administration and data analysis.

3. Develop specifications for the role of a "good student."
Ans-Student should be

1. studios

2. honest

3. punctual

4. eager to learn

5. hungry for the knowledge

4. What are the criticisms of SERVQUAL? What are its developers' responses to these criticisms?

Ans- Notwithstanding its growing popularity and widespread application, SERVQUAL has been subjected to a number of theoretical and operational criticisms which are detailed below:

(1) Theoretical:
- Paradigmatic objections: SERVQUAL is based on a disconfirmation paradigm rather than an attitudinal paradigm; and SERVQUAL fails to draw on established economic, statistical and psychological theory.
- Gaps model: there is little evidence that customers/clients assess service quality in terms of P – E gaps.
- Process orientation: SERVQUAL focuses on the process of service delivery, not the outcomes of the service encounter.
- Dimensionality: SERVQUAL's five dimensions are not universals; the number of dimensions comprising SQ is contextualized; items do not always load on to the factors which one would a priori expect; and there is a high degree of inter correlation between the five RATER dimensions.

(2) Operational:

- Expectations: the term expectation is polysemic; consumers use standards other than expectations to evaluate SQ; and SERVQUAL fails to measure absolute SQ expectations.
- Item composition: four or five items cannot capture the variability within each SQ dimension.
- Moments of truth (MOT): customers/clients' assessments of SQ may vary from MOT to MOT.
- Polarity: the reversed polarity of items in the scale causes respondent error.
- Scale points: the seven-point Likert scale is flawed.
- Two administrations: two administrations of the instrument causes boredom and confusion.
- Variance extracted: the over SERVQUAL score accounts for a disappointing proportion of item variances.

CHAPTER 8 - SERVICE FAILURES AND RECOVERY STRATEGIES

DISCUSSION QUESTIONS:

1. Discuss the following types of complaints: instrumental, noninstrumental, ostensive, and reflexive

Ans- Basically, a complaint is grievance that can be defined in the form of disappointment, misery, and disdain about something. In the same manner, a complaint reflects dissatisfaction or disappointment in relation to object or person. Instrumental, non-instrumental, ostensive, and reflexive are the main categories of complaints. For example, instrumental complaints are communicated with the end goal of changing an undesirable state of issues. Moreover, it is also found that, instrumental complaints make up just a little number of a great many grievances that are voiced consistently. Then again, non-instrumental complaints are communicated without desire that an undesirable state will be adjusted. For example, these sorts of grumblings are significantly more voiced as stand in comparison to instrumental grievances and according to this an undesirable state will be changed. Along with this, ostensive complaints are coordinated at somebody or something outside the domain of the grumbler.

2. What is the service recovery paradox? Provide an example based on your own personal experience

Ans- The **service recovery paradox (SRP)** is a situation in which a customer thinks more highly of a company after the company has corrected a problem with their service, compared to how they would regard the company if non-faulty service had been provided. The main reason behind this thinking is that successful recovery of a faulty service increases the assurance and confidence from the customer.

For example, a traveler's flight is cancelled. When she calls the airline, they apologise and offer her another flight of her choice on the same day, and a discount voucher against future travel. Under the service recovery paradox, the traveler is now *happier* with the airline, and more loyal to it, than she would have been had no problem occurred.

Understanding SRP has been an important goal for both research/studyers and managers/stakeholders, as service failure is one of the main determinants of customer switching behavior and successful recovery from these failures is seen by some as critical for customer retention. Recovery is especially important for service providers for whom ensuring an error-free service is impossible.

3. Discuss the following types of failure outcomes: voice, exit, and retaliation.

Ans-Voice marketing

Voice marketing is a set of strategies and tactics used to reach target audiences through the use of various voice-enabled devices powered by voice assistants. As you can see, the potential for voice marketing is vast due to its ability to be at virtually every touch point of your customer's journey.

Exit

Exit strategies are techniques used by companies to abandon products, divisions, or even entire industries. Exit strategies are implemented when a company decides that it is no longer beneficial to remain active in a given market or industry. For example, a company that manufactures men's suits may determine that it wants to jettison its leisure suit division because of declining sales and a vanishing market. Or, a U.S. electronics producer might decide to exit the entire industry because of pressure from less expensive imports. Exit strategies may also be employed by business owners, who must decide at what point and under what circumstances they will cede control of their businesses to others.

Retaliation

Retaliation is an aggressive behavior engaged in with the intention of getting even (Huefner & Hunt 2000; Myers 1990). Although aggressive behavior has long been investigated in the organizational behavior discipline, it has only recently been investigated in the customer behavior discipline (Grandey, Dickter & Sin 2004; Harris & Reynolds 2003; Reynolds & Harris 2006). In a customer context, retaliation can be both overt and covert and includes behaviours such as verbal or physical abuse, theft, creating a cost/loss, vandalism, and trashing (Huefner & Hunt 2000). Retaliatory behavior has a single motive: to correct some perceived inequity (Skarlicki & Folger 1007). This inequity is primarily psychological: it's a case of 'You got me. I got you back. Now we're even' (Huefner & Hunt 2000: 62).

4. What are the pros and cons of complaining customers/clients

Ans- Some key advantages of customer complaints are:

- Complaints **highlight key areas where your products or services** need improvement.
- Customer complaints **open opportunities for your team to have honest discussions with your customers/clients.** These conversations can help customers/clients feel like the vital components to your success.
- Customer complaints provide **valuable insights into how trained your front line support is and how to improve them.** They can be used as training models for new team members.

Disadvantages of customer complaints is hearing negative reviews about a product that you've put your all into and are passionate about. However, while it's not always a good feeling to receive complaints, remember that no business is ever perfect no matter how many changes they make, and that there are a ton of **benefits of customer complaints.**

CHAPTER 9 - CUSTOMER RETENTION

DISCUSSION QUESTIONS

1. Why has conquest marketing become an acceptable form of business for many of today's firms?

Ans- Your service department is absolutely the most effective conquest opportunity you have. In fact, there is an entire industry dedicated to this customer need. You can service almost any car at your dealership. Target the customers/clients you want. Obviously it makes sense to target people driving the cars you sell, but what about targeting those you wish to sell to.

For instance, a Honda dealer can target a current Kia customer with an incredible service special. Once they get to the dealership, you can try and determine their equity position and make them an awesome deal. If they don't bite, no problem. You are creating an extremely valuable marketing list. If they do, you traded on a competitive make, and you could also be building up a used car fleet for another conquest campaign (more on that in a minute).

Going back to conquest strategy development, think about how you can solve a problem. Look at competitive sales within a short distance to your dealership. Convenience is a huge factor when it comes to servicing your car. Think about what you can offer to make people's lives easier.

2. How have changes within service distribution channels impacted customer retention?

Ans- Making your offering available to more customers/clients is one of the most solid growth strategies. Many companies get stuck with the same distribution model for decades, although it might be obvious that a change is needed. The most common reason for the status quo: channel conflict. Distribution partners don't like competition. They want exclusive products and always better prices. In the case of family-owned businesses distribution has been built on personal relationship so the decision to expand is even more difficult to make.

3. Discuss the distinction between zero defects and zero nonconformities.

Ans- We have had some rather good discussions on the difference between zero defectives and zero nonconformities. You will find some links at the bottom of the page that might be helpful.

The idea that a supplier is going to provide zero nonconformities is really wishful thinking in a non-reality world. Zero defects however is achievable in the real world. The difference is subtle but easily explainable.

Let's say you are asked to make three white cars. You make one red. That is a nonconformance because it doesn't meet the requirements. It is not a defect though because the car is in perfect, usable condition.

In our business, we coat a specific number of threads on a fastener. Let's say the spec is 3 to 5 threads. If we coat 5 1/8 threads, it is "out-of-spec" and a nonconformance. The part is not a defect though and may perform better than the ones in spec.

Most suppliers could meet a "Zero Defects" requirement if it weren't being misinterpreted as meaning "Zero Nonconformance".

4. Discuss the characteristics of successful guarantees.

Ans-

- Unconditional – The guarantee should make its promise unconditionally – no strings attached
- Meaningful – The firm should guarantee elements of the service that are important to the customer – The payout should cover fully the customer's dissatisfaction
- Easy to Understand – Customers/clients need to understand what to expect – Employees/staffs need to understand what to do
- Easy to Invoke – The firm should eliminate hoops or red tape in the way of accessing or collecting on the guarantee

CHAPTER 10 - PUTTING TOGETHER: CREATING THE SEAMLESS SERVICE FIRM

DISCUSSION QUESTIONS

1. Discuss seamlessness as it relates to "tooth-to-tail" performance.

Ans- It is projected that the Department of Defense (DoD) will see a funding reduction of $487 billion over the next 10 years (Office of Management and Budget [OMB], 2013). In order to stay within budget, the DoD plans to implement targeted reductions in force structure, reprioritize key missions and the requirements that support them, promote efficiency improvements in acquisition, and continue to reform other business practices. However, these efforts, at least in their current form, will prove insufficient. The Congressional Budget Office (CBO) asserts that the DoD s costs will soon outstrip its budget as expenditures for manpower, maintenance, and health care continue to increase, thereby eliminating the funds necessary for the planned recapitalization, modernization, and transformation of the military (CBO, 2013). The DoD must make hard decisions in order to prevent such an outlook from becoming a reality. In the past, the DoD has reduced the number of military personnel (and to a lesser extent, equipment orders and program funding) in order to constrain costs. At present, however, the active military force structure is already near an all-time low, and existing equipment inventories are becoming older, smaller, and less effective against emerging technologies. It is within this challenging environment that the DoD must strive to improve its tooth-to-tail ratio. This term, familiar to defense analysts, refers to the relative level of support personnel (military, civilian, and contractor) required to maintain combat forces. The tooth refers to the personnel that train for and perform operational missions, whereas the tail refers to the personnel that support the combat forces. As of 2011, the active-duty military end-strength was 1,459,409 (BLS, 2012). Of these personnel, only 17% are identified as performing combat specialties.

2. Discuss each tier of the three-tiered model of service firms separately and then as a combined unit.

Ans- Success is based on the effective management and integration of the customer tier, the boundary tier, and a coordination tier. The Customer Tier focuses on customer expectations, needs, and competencies. The Boundary Tier concerns itself with the individuals who interact with the customers/clients--the boundary spanners. Service personnel in the boundary tier must be more flexible, communicative, able to deal with stress, and willing to take the initiative than their Manufacturing/Production counterparts. Ultimately, boundary spanning personnel are only as good as the non personal aspects of the service delivery system that supports their efforts. The Coordination Tier is the responsibility of upper management and involves coordinating the activities that help integrate the customer and the boundary tiers. The primary challenge of the coordination tier is to get the various departments within the organization to work with one common goal in mind--serving the customer.

3. What is the importance of organizational culture?

Ans- A common platform where individuals work in unison to earn profits as well as a livelihood for themselves is called an organization. A place where individuals realize the dream of making it big is called an organization. Every organization has its unique style of working which often contributes to its culture. The beliefs, ideologies, principles and values of an organization form its culture. The culture of the workplace controls the way employees/staffs behave amongst themselves as well as with people outside the organization.

- **The culture decides the way employees/staffs interact at their workplace.** A healthy culture encourages the employees/staffs to stay motivated and loyal towards the management.

- **The culture of the workplace also goes a long way in promoting healthy competition at the workplace.** Employees/staffs try their level best to perform better than their fellow workers and earn recognition and appreciation of the superiors. It is the culture of the workplace which actually motivates the employees/staffs to perform.

- Every organization must have set guidelines for the employees/staffs to work accordingly. **The culture of an organization represents certain predefined policies which guide the employees/staffs and give them a sense of direction at the workplace.** Every individual is clear about his roles and responsibilities in the organization and know how to accomplish the tasks ahead of the deadlines.

- No two organizations can have the same work culture. It is the culture of an organization which makes it distinct from others. **The work culture goes a long way in creating the brand image of the organization**. The work culture gives an identity to the organization. In other words, an organization is known by its culture.

- **The organization culture brings all the employees/staffs on a common platform**. The employees/staffs must be treated equally and no one should feel neglected or left out at the workplace. It is essential for the employees/staffs to adjust well in the organization culture for them to deliver their level best.

- **The work culture unites the employees/staffs who are otherwise from different back grounds**, families and have varied attitudes and mentalities. The culture gives the employees/staffs a sense of unity at the workplace.

  Certain organizations follow a culture where all the employees/staffs irrespective of their designations have to step into the office on time. Such a culture encourages the employees/staffs to be punctual which eventually benefits them in the long run. It is the culture of the organization which makes the individuals a successful professional.

- Every employee is clear with his roles and responsibilities and strives hard to accomplish the tasks within the desired time frame as per the set guidelines. Implementation of policies is never a problem in organizations where people follow a set culture. The new employees/staffs also try their level best to understand the work culture and make the organization a better place to work.

- **The work culture promotes healthy relationship amongst the employees/staffs**. No one treats work as a burden and moulds himself according to the culture.

- **It is the culture of the organization which extracts the best out of each team member**. In a culture where management is very particular about the reporting system, the employees/staffs however busy they are would send their reports by end of the day. No one has to force anyone to work. The culture develops a habit in the individuals which makes them successful at the workplace.

4.What are the key components of a service audit?
- Research/study the Audit Area. It is essential to understand the **business process** or function to be audited.
- Maintain Open Communications Throughout the Planning **Process**.
- Conduct **Process** Walk-Throughs.
- Map Risks to the Organization, **Process**, or Function & Obtain Data Prior to Fieldwork.

CHAPTER 11 - SERVICE DELIVERY PROCESS

DISCUSSION QUESTIONS

1. Explain how the inability to inventory services affects the operational efficiency of most service firms

Ans- The firms provide the facility of many services in the operation department. The new technique is important for analyze the inventory services. The firms operate the inventory services according to input and output. Inventory services provide the good quality of the product. The product should be in the good life cycle because it focus on the input and output services.

2. Compare Thompson's perfect-world model to the focused factory and plant-within-a-plant concepts

Ans- Thompson's Perfect-World-Model, Focused Factory, and Plant- Within- a- Plant Concept All these models are known as the efficiency models of services, and differ with each other in terms of their structure, application, and aspects. Thompson's Perfect World Model began from the technical core of the company, whereas focused factor concentrates on a specific job. Technical core refers to a place of a firm where its key operations take place. For instance, kitchen is a technical core of a restaurant. In accordance to Thompson's Perfect-World Model to operate efficiently, a firm must be able to operate "as if the market will take up the particular kind of product at an incessant rate and as if the inputs flowed unceasingly at a stable rate and with specific quality." The argument given by Thompson depict that uncertainty create inefficiency. So, with absence of uncertainty, decisions with the core can be programmes and individual discretion can be replaced by rules (Hoffman & Bateson, 2010). As per the model given by Thompson, a system without uncertainty is easy to control and manage, but it is impossible to attain. All companies trade off against the ideal operations demands. This trade-off can be attained with the help of focused factory. This model concentrates on a specific job.

3. What is buffering? How do the strategies of anticipating, smoothing, and rationing relate to buffering?

Ans- Preloading or loading of the data be it any kind of data in order to view it or process it for the required task is called buffering. The audio or video files use buffering the procedure a the most, it is to buffer or preload the data in advance to certain extent before playing or listening to the same. The advantage of the same is to load a certain data so that there is no interruption or disruption when the data is being viewed or processed which can be due to any delay in the transmission or loss of connectivity. Smoothing, anticipating and rationing are certain alternatives to buffering as stated by Thompson, anticipating and smoothing are the focus on the uncertainty.

4. Discuss some specific examples of how the customer's involvement in the service encounter influences the operational efficiency of the average service firm.

Ans- A service encounter is that period of time during which the customer and the service firm interact in person over telephone or through other media (Shostack 1985). Essentially, a service encounter has been defined as a social interaction involving one human being interacting with another (Czepiel et al. 1985). Given the high degree of person-to-person inter action and, quite frequently the absence of an exchange of tangible goods, the service encounter becomes a critical component of service quality. There are three key players involved in a service encounter that shape the outcome of any encounter: the service firm, which sets policies and guidelines; the employees/staffs, who enact the policies of the firm; and the customer, who seeks to satisfy a range of needs and wants. Chandon et al. (1997) propose several service encounter dimensions on the basis of which a service encounter can be assessed. These dimensions and their subcategories differ depending on whether it is the customer or the firm doing the assessment. From the customer's view, the service provider's perceived competence (expertise), listening skills and dedication are likely to be key in assessing the service received. From the employee's view, 110 The service encounter customer courtesy, efficiency in terms of getting the transaction completed and personal (employee) satisfaction are likely to be key in the assessment process. Original work by Czepiel et al. (1985) identified seven key characteristics of a service encounter that can be considered the distinguishing factors when analyzing service encounters. Briefly, service encounters usually • are goal oriented • are undertaken as part of work activities • are primarily a stranger relationship • are narrow in scope: only surface topics of conversation • are mostly task oriented • mostly follow a pre-defined set of rules to facilitate the interaction • involve the roles of service provider and client (customer) It is probably true to say that service encounters are alike in that they have certain common distinguishing characteristics; however, due to the dynamic nature of human interactions, every encounter differs to some degree. Many service encounters have been considered in isolation in that they have been considered outside a broader context. Often when research/studyers consider service encounters, they merely think about individual events rather than connections between them. While much research/study has focused on discrete service encounters, more recent studies have examined multiple service encounters, or sequences of events. For example, Verhoef et al. (2004) approached the service encounter as a sequence of events. In particular, they tested a model on how events contribute to an overall evaluation of a sequence of events and found that while the average performance during the encounter is important, peak performances are critical for satisfaction formation. Thus, from a managerial point of view, it is important not only to manage the overall performance of the service encounter but also to generate a number of positive peak performances. Apart from peak performances, the performance trend – that is whether positive or negative performances are first or last in the sequence as well as the quality of the final performance in a service sequence – also significantly impacts customer evaluations (Hansen and Danaher 1999). In a hotel context, management has not only to be mindful of the average quality of the encounters a hotel guest has with various staff for the check-in process (e.g. porter, check-in clerk and bell boy) but also ensure that unexpected extras, for example, can lead to perceived peak performances from the customer's point of view.

5. Discuss the steps for developing a meaningful blueprint

Ans- Effective service blueprinting follows five key high-level steps:

1. **Find support:** Build a core cross disciplinary team and establish stakeholder support.
2. **Define the goal:** Define the scope and align on the goal of the blueprinting initiative.
3. **Gather research/study:** Gather research/study from customers/clients, employees/staffs, and stakeholders using a variety of methods.
4. **Map the blueprint:** Use this research/study to fill in a low-fidelity blueprint.
5. **Refine and distribute:** Add additional content and refine towards a high-fidelity blueprint that can be distributed amongst clients and stakeholders.

CHAPTER 12 - THE PRICING OF SERVICES

DISCUSSION QUESTIONS

1. What factors comprise consumer perceptions of value?

Ans-Factors compromise consumer perceptions of value

Service Quality
This is extremely important because customers/clients who have a negative experience with a company's customer service center rarely return to make additional purchases in the future. Focus on how well customer service interactions were resolved (and if they were resolved). What do your customers/clients think in terms of the knowledge and dependability of your brand when they needed assistance? How long did it take to help resolve any issues? Don't forget that customer service reps should be proactive with their interactions and solutions.

Reputation
Potential customers/clients will more than likely do their research/study about which company they will do business with. It's important to know what your past customers/clients have said about their experience with your company. This will affect how new customers/clients perceive your brand. This includes aspects such as whether or not people view your company as one that stands behind its customers/clients and were problems successfully resolved in a professional and timely manner.

Customer Experience
Obviously, customer experience can drastically affect others perceptions about your company. Focus on how were previous customer interactions resolved. This can also include a customer's previous experience with your company's products or services, your prices or fees compared to your competitors and the quality / value of your products, services or interactions with your company.

Consistency
Consistency between interactions with your company across multiple ways of communication can have a lasting effect on customer perception. Customers/clients should know what to expect from your company when they reach out, no matter the means of communication. If they contact customer service, they should know what to expect no matter who they talk to. This is why having real-time data available to all customer service agents is so important. Also, although automated chatbots are great in certain situations, some customers/clients will prefer human interaction.

Value
Customers/clients should feel valued when they contact your company. After all, they are the reason your company is in business. A customer's time and money should be worth what they get back in terms of services, products they purchase and the

experience they have. So what kind of value does your company offer to its customers/clients?
Customer perception is vital to customer retention and brand loyalty. If customers/clients trust your company, they will return to make additional purchases, refer others and leave positive reviews online, all of which can affect your customers/clients' future decisions.

2. Discuss the role of price as an indicator of quality to consumers.
Ans- One of the intriguing aspects of pricing is that buyers are likely to use price as an indicator of both service costs and service quality—price is at once an attraction variable and a repellent. Customers/clients' use of price as an indicator of quality depends on several factors, one of which is the other information available to them.

When service cues to quality are readily accessible, when brand names provide evidence of a company's reputation, or when level of advertising communicates the company's belief in the brand, customers/clients may prefer to use those cues instead of price.

In other situations, however, such as when quality is hard to detect or when quality or price varies a great deal within a class of services, consumers may believe that price is the best indicator of quality.

Many of these conditions typify situations that face consumers when purchasing services. Another factor that increases the dependence on price as a quality indicator is the risk associated with the service purchase. In high-risk situations, many of which involve credence services such as medical treatment or management consulting, the customer will look to price as a surrogate for quality.

Because customers/clients depend on price as a cue to quality and because price sets expectations of quality, service prices must be determined carefully. In addition to chosen to cover costs or match competitors, prices must be chosen to convey appropriate quality signal.

Pricing too low can lead to inaccurate inferences about the quality of the service. Pricing too high can set expectations that may be difficult to match in service delivery. Because goods are dominated by search properties, price is not used to judge quality as often as it is in services, where experience and credence properties dominate. Any services marketer must be aware of the signals that price conveys about its offerings.

3. Should self-service always be rewarded with lower prices? Please explain.

Ans- Customer self-service is any activity where the customer performs work on their own behalf without the assistance of company staff. The term applies to a wide range of activities — from customers/clients picking their own groceries to searching an online help center for answers to their questions. As modern companies aim to serve huge customer bases with relatively small teams, self-service portals, knowledge-bases, and online preferences and account tools have seen significant numbers of tasks shift from company-driven to customer-driven.

4. Under what conditions is price segmentation most effective?

Ans- With a price segmentation strategy, you offer the same product at different prices to different groups. If you operate a product segmentation strategy, you offer different versions of a product to different groups. Segmentation is most effective when you can identify clear differences in market requirements.

CHAPTER 13 - DEVELOPING THE SERVICE COMMUNICATION MIX

DISCUSSION QUESTIONS

I. Discuss the options available for positioning and differentiating service firms.

Ans- **Positioning** is a strategic process that marketers use to determine the place or "niche" an offering should occupy in a given market, relative to other customer alternatives. When you position a product or service, you answer these questions:
- **Place**: What place does the offering occupy in its market?
- **Rank**: How does the product or service fare against its competitors in the areas evaluated by customers/clients deciding what to buy?
- **Attitude**: How do we want customers/clients to think about this offering and the benefits it offers them?
- **Outcomes**: What must we do to ensure the product or service delivers on the positioning we select?

Marketers use the positioning process to identify the distinctive place they want a product or service to hold in the minds of a target market segment. Effective positioning is always aimed at a specific target segment. In fact, positioning tailors the generally focused value proposition to the needs and interests of a particular target segment.

Differentiation is closely related to positioning. Differentiation is the process companies use to make a product or service stand out from its competitors in ways that provide unique value to the customer. Differentiation identifies a set of characteristics and benefits that make a product different and better for a target audience. Ideally these qualities are things that 1) customers/clients value when they are evaluating choices in a purchasing decision, and 2) competitors cannot easily copy. When both conditions exist, the offering is more attractive to target customers/clients.

Differentiation is at work any time you're choosing between two products in the same category. For example, when you're buying a soft drink, why do you choose Coke, Pepsi, Sprite, or Mountain Dew? Is it because of the taste? The cost? The level of sugar or caffeine? Or is it something less tangible, like the way you just want to smile when you drink Coke, or you feel amped up when you drink Mountain Dew? These tangible and intangible qualities are what differentiate one soft drink from another.

2. Describe the strategic differences among the four elements of the communications mix.

Ans- A marketing communications mix is the same as a promotion mix and is just another term for promotion mix. There are five marketing communications to put into the mix: Advertising, Sales Promotion, Public Relations, Personal Selling, and Direct Marketing. This basically all boils down to a mix of promotional efforts to bring in sales and increase brand equity.

Advertising – Any paid form of non personal presentation and promotion of ideas, goods, or services by an identified sponsor.

Personal selling – Personal presentation by the firm's sales force for the purpose of making sales and building customer relationships.

Sales promotion – Short-term incentives to encourage the purchase or sale of a product or service.

Public relations – Building good relationships with the company's various publics by obtaining favorable publicity, building up a good "corporate image", and handling or heading off unfavorable rumors, stories, and events.

Direct marketing – Direct communications with carefully targeted individual consumers to obtain an immediate response and cultivate lasting customer relationships.

4. What is the relevance of the rational mathematician model as it relates to developing communications strategy

Ans- A mathematical model is a description of a system using mathematical concepts and language. The process of developing a mathematical model is termed mathematical modeling. Mathematical models are used in the natural sciences (such as physics, biology, earth science, chemistry) and engineering/production disciplines (such as computer science, electrical engineering/production), as well as in non-physical systems such as the social sciences (such as economics, psychology, sociology, political science). Mathematical models are also used in music[1], linguistics[2] and philosophy (for example, intensively in analytic philosophy).

A model may help to explain a system and to study the effects of different components, and to make predictions about behavior.

Mathematical models can take many forms, including dynamical systems, statistical models, differential equations, or game theoretic models. These and other types of models can overlap, with a given model involving a variety of abstract structures. In general, mathematical models may include logical models. In many cases, the quality of a scientific field depends on how well the mathematical models developed on the theoretical side agree with results of repeatable experiments. Lack of agreement between theoretical mathematical models and experimental measurements often leads to important advances as better theories are developed.

In the physical sciences, a traditional mathematical model contains most of the following elements:

- Governing equations
- Supplementary sub-models
- Defining equations
- Constitutive equations
- Assumptions and constraints
- Initial and boundary conditions
- Classical constraints and kinematic equations

5. Why should service employees/staffs be considered when developing communications materials?

Ans- A communication strategy is the critical piece bridging the situation analysis and the implementation of a social and behavior change communication (SBCC) program. It is a written plan that details how an SBCC program will reach its vision, given the current situation. Effective communication strategies use a systematic process and behavioral theory to design and implement communication activities that encourage sustainable social and behavior change.

Most communication strategies include the following elements:

- Brief summary of the situation analysis
- Audience segmentation
- Program theory to inform strategy development
- Communication objectives
- Approaches for achieving objectives
- Positioning for the desired change
- Benefits and messages to encourage desired change
- Communication channels to disseminate messages
- Implementation plan
- Monitoring and evaluation plan
- Budgets

CHAPTER 14 - MANAGING THE FIRMS PHYSICAL EVIDENCE

DISCUSSION QUESTIONS

1.Discuss the strategic role of physical evidence.
Ans-Physical evidence is composed of three categories

   1. **Facility exterior**

   2. **Facility interior**

   3. **Other tangibles**

- The extensive use of physical evidence varies by the type of service firm
- All service firms used to recognize the importance of managing their physical evidence in its multifaceted role of:

   1. Packaging the service

   2. Facilitating the flow of the service delivery process

   3. Socializing customers/clients and employees/staffs alike in terms of their respective roles, behaviors, and relationships

   4. Differentiating the firm from its competitors

2. Discuss the relevance of remote, self-service, and interpersonal services to facility design.
Ans-
Remote- has little or no customer involvement with the service scape.
Self service- customer performs most of the activities and few if any employees/staffs are involved.
Interpersonal services- placed between two extremes and represent situations in which both the customer and the employee are present and active in the service scape.

3. Discuss internal responses to the firm's environment.

Ans- An organization's *internal environment* is composed of the elements within the organization, including current employees/staffs, management, and especially corporate culture, which defines employee behavior. Although some elements affect the organization as a whole, others affect only the manager. A manager's philosophical or leadership style directly impacts employees/staffs. Traditional managers/stakeholders give explicit instructions to employees/staffs, while progressive managers/stakeholders empower employees/staffs to make many of their own decisions. Changes in philosophy and/or leadership style are under the control of the manager. The following sections describe some of the elements that make up the internal environment.

An organization's **mission statement** describes what the organization stands for and why it exists. It explains the overall purpose of the organization and includes the attributes that distinguish it from other organizations of its type.

A mission statement should be more than words on a piece of paper; it should reveal a company's philosophy, as well as its purpose. This declaration should be a living, breathing document that provides information and inspiration for the members of the organization. A mission statement should answer the questions, "What are our values?" and "What do we stand for?" This statement provides focus for an organization by rallying its members to work together to achieve its common goals.

But not all mission statements are effective in America's businesses. Effective mission statements lead to effective efforts. In today's quality-conscious and highly competitive environments, an effective mission statement's purpose is centered on serving the needs of customers/clients. A good mission statement is precise in identifying the following intents of a company:

Customers/clients — who will be served

Products/services — what will be produced

Location — where the products/services will be produced

Philosophy — what ideology will be followed

Company policies are guidelines that govern how certain organizational situations are addressed. Just as colleges maintain policies about admittance, grade appeals, prerequisites, and waivers, companies establish policies to provide guidance to managers/stakeholders who must make decisions about circumstances that occur frequently within their organization. Company policies are an indication of an organization's personality and should coincide with its mission statement.

The **formal structure** of an organization is the hierarchical arrangement of tasks and people. This structure determines how information flows within the organization, which departments are responsible for which activities, and where the decision-making power rests.

Some organizations use a chart to simplify the breakdown of its formal structure. This **organizational chart** is a pictorial display of the official lines of authority and communication within an organization.

The **organizational culture** is an organization's personality. Just as each person has a distinct personality, so does each organization. The culture of an organization distinguishes it from others and shapes the actions of its members.

Four main components make up an organization's culture:

Values

Heroes

Rites and rituals

Social network

Values are the basic beliefs that define employees/staffs' successes in an organization. For example, many universities place high values on professors being published. If a faculty member is published in a professional journal, for example, his or her chances of receiving tenure may be enhanced. The university wants to ensure that a published professor stays with the university for the duration of his or her academic career — and this professor's ability to write for publications is a value.

The second component is heroes. A *hero* is an exemplary person who reflects the image, attitudes, or values of the organization and serves as a role model to other employees/staffs. A hero is sometimes the founder of the organization (think Sam Walton of Wal-Mart). However, the hero of a company doesn't have to be the founder; it can be an everyday worker, such as hard-working paralegal Erin Brockovich, who had a tremendous impact on the organization.

Rites and rituals, the third component, are routines or ceremonies that the company uses to recognize high-performing employees/staffs. Awards banquets, company gatherings, and quarterly meetings can acknowledge distinguished employees/staffs for outstanding service. The honorees are meant to exemplify and inspire all employees/staffs of the company during the rest of the year.

The final component, the *social network,* is the informal means of communication within an organization. This network, sometimes referred to as the company grapevine, carries the stories of both heroes and those who have failed. It is through this network that employees/staffs really learn about the organization's culture and values.

A byproduct of the company's culture is the **organizational climate.** The overall tone of the workplace and the morale of its workers are elements of daily climate. Worker attitudes dictate the positive or negative "atmosphere" of the workplace. The daily relationships and interactions of employees/staffs are indicative of an organization's climate.

Resources are the people, information, facilities, infrastructure, machinery, equipment, supplies, and finances at an organization's disposal. People are the paramount resource of all organizations. Information, facilities, machinery equipment, materials, supplies, and finances are supporting, nonhuman resources that complement workers in their quests to accomplish the organization's mission statement. The availability of resources and the way that managers/stakeholders value the human and nonhuman resources impact the organization's environment.

4.What is the impact of music on customer and employee behavior?

Ans- This article examines the effects of music on consumers' reactions to waiting for services. An experimental study was conducted to test three different constructs — perceived wait duration, emotional evaluation of the service environment and emotional response to the wait—as mediators between music and behavioral response to the service organization. Results of the study showed that, regardless of its valence, music ameliorates emotional evaluation of the service environment which in turn positively affects approach behavior towards the service organization. Furthermore, positively valanced music triggers a more positive emotional response to the wait and a stronger approach behavior towards the service organization than negatively valanced music. Although positively valanced music also increases perceived wait duration, the latter does not have a significant effect on consumers' behavioral response to the service organization.

5. Develop strategies for a service firm that would enhance the firm's touch and taste appeals.

Ans- Though the retail industry continues to face pressure from e-commerce, several brands have done a great job of enhancing their businesses and brands through brick-and-mortar stores. Major brands like Starbuck's®, Pottery Barn® and Anthropologie have survived and even thrived by creating a unique experience.

These retailers have the strength of dedicated merchandising teams, but that doesn't mean that small independent stores can't borrow some of their best ideas. Their ideas and tactics all have one thing in common; they create a unique experience for the customer and appeal to one of their five senses. To intrigue customers/clients and create a powerful experience like these successful brands it is important to appeal to a customer's sense of taste, sight, touch, smell, and hearing.

Here are some ways owners of independent custom frame shops can incorporate merchandising tactics used by some of the country's top retailers. To get started, begin with your target customer in mind to help you develop a framework to work from. Develop a customer profile in writing and include which big brands also target this customer.

CHAPTER 15 - PEOPLE ISSUES MANAGING SERVICE EMPLOYEES/STAFFS

DISCUSSION QUESTIONS

1. Relate the concepts of intangibility, inseparability, heterogeneity, and perish ability to the importance of personnel in the service firm.

Ans- Intangibility makes it difficult to experience a service before purchasing it. Heterogeneity and intangibility make word-of-mouth communication an important means of promotion. The prices of services are based on task performance, time required, or demand. Perish ability creates difficulties in balancing supply and demand because unused capacity cannot be stored. The point in time when a significant number of customers/clients desire a service is called peak demand; demand-based pricing results in higher prices charged for services during peak demand. When services are offered in a bundle, marketers must decide whether to offer them at one price, price them separately, or use a combination of the two methods. Because services are intangible, customers/clients may rely on price as a sign of quality. For some services, market conditions may dictate the price; for others, state and local government regulations may limit price flexibility.

2. How can marketing be utilized to reduce the amount of stress and conflict experienced by boundary-spanning personnel?

Ans- Three types of customer-oriented boundary-spanning behaviors (COBSBs) a frontline service employee may perform that are associated with linking a service organization to its potential or actual customers/clients: external representation, internal influence, and service delivery. The authors propose and test a withdrawal model to explain the negative effects of role conflict and role ambiguity on COBSBs across a sample of 220 lower-level, nonprofessional service providers of a major retail bank and a sample of 90 higher-level, professional service providers from the business credit division of an international financial services corporation. The results demonstrate that (1) indirect paths through job satisfaction and organizational commitment entirely account for the negative effects of the role stressors on COBSBs, (2) the indirect negative effects of the role stressors are stronger on external representation and internal influence behaviors, and (3) role conflict also has a significant positive direct relationship with internal influence behaviors.

3. What is climate? Why is organizational climate of particular importance to service firms?

Ans- Organizational climate concerns the policies and practices of an organization or unit of an organization. It concerns the behaviors that are encouraged and supported. It is communicated in several ways.

Policies: These are the written rules for the behaviors that people should and should not do. Policies describe how things should be done.

Practices: These are the behaviors that employees/staffs and their supervisors engage in, in other words, how policies are or are not enacted.

What is encouraged and discouraged. These are the expectations that supervisors and other employees/staffs express about what each employee should and should not do. For Beth is was customer service and for Mike it was efficiency.

Where the rewards are. Nothing expresses expectations like rewards. These can be monetary, such as bonuses for high sales volume, or nonmonetary, such as praise for a job well done.

Climate is important because employees/staffs are likely to engage in the behaviors that are encouraged. In Mike's company the emphasis is on efficiency and productivity, so that focuses employee attention in those areas. Employees/staffs are likely to adopt an efficiency/productivity mindset that guides their interactions with others and their work. In Beth's company, the emphasis is on customer service. There will be less focus on efficiency/productivity and more on serving customer needs. If a potential customer leaves a message, Beth is likely to call back right away and will be patient if the customer is long winded on the phone. Mike, on the other hand, will be more strategic in how he spends time, and he might not be in a hurry to return the call if he does not believe the customer is a good prospect. The amount a customer is likely to purchase will determine the time he is willing to invest.

Companies can use climate to encourage the behaviors they wish from their employees/staffs. To a great extent climate is encouraged by the sorts of issues and problems the company deals with. For example, financial services companies are likely to develop strong ethical climates that discourage unethical or illegal acts involving money. Construction companies, where people work with dangerous machinery, are likely to develop strong safety climates. Even within the same organization, there can be department differences in what is emphasized. In a Manufacturing/Production company, for example, ethical climate is highly relevant to the accounting department and safety climate to the assembly plants.

4.Define enfranchisernent. Summarize the seven tests of reward effectiveness.

Ans- the fact of giving a person or group of people the right to vote in elections:

- New models of democratic enfranchisement are needed.
- Redrawing voting districts addresses the issue of voter enfranchisement.

Schneider and Bowen (*Winning the Service Game.* HBS Press, 1995) say that there are four ways organizations fail to use reward effectively.

- They fail to use the full range of available rewards. Incidentally, pay fails the test of an effective reward.

- They fail to use the intrinsic reward of goal accomplishment. If a customer leaves with a big smile, it can be highly rewarding to the employee.

- They fail to use reward systems to facilitate service quality. The reward system may inhibit rather than facilitate. Remember "the folly of rewarding A while hoping for B." People do the things that are more likely to lead to rewards or less likely to lead to punishment. Behavior that yields rewards will persist. Behavior that fails to yield results will be extinguished.

- They fail to manage reward systems effectively. Sometimes rewards or uneven or inequitable.

CHAPTER 16 - PEOPLE ISSUES MANAGING SERVICE CONSUMERS

DISCUSSION QUESTIONS

1. Discuss the pros and cons of increasing customer participation in the service delivery process.

Ans - Increasing customer participation is associated with a number of advantages and disadvantages. The primary advantage to the customer and the service firm is that customers/clients can customize their own service and produce it faster and less expensively than if the firm had produced it. Customers/clients who pump their own gas, make their own salads, and pick their own strawberries are classic examples. On the other hand, increased levels of customer participation are also associated with the firm's losing control of quality, increased waste, which increases operating costs, and customer perceptions that the firm may be attempting to distance itself from its customers/clients.

2. Select four of the eight "principles of waiting and discuss their significance to managing the consumer's experience.

Ans-**Principles of waiting**

1 – Unoccupied Time Feels Longer than Occupied Time

Experience designers should ensure that appropriate tasks or entertainment are provided for individuals who must wait. Magazines in medical and dental waiting rooms are a great example of this. Similarly, televisions are used in many locations where people need to wait.

2 – Pre and Post-process Waits Feel Longer than In-process Waits

Because waiting feels less onerous once someone is already involved in a process, experience designers should initiate processes as soon as possible. It's better to have a longer overall process with waiting within the process, than a very quick process with waiting either side of it. A simple example of this could be requesting a customer to complete a form as soon as they enter a location. This activity brings them "in-process", reducing the sense of waiting that they feel for the remainder of their experience. Again, medical practices often do this.

3 – Anxiety Makes Waits Seem Longer

Anxiety causes people to feel that time moves more slowly and makes waiting seem longer. To overcome this, experience designers should create calming waiting spaces. This can be achieved through furnishing, color palette choice and music. Using relaxing furniture, calming colors and soothing music can reduce the sense of waiting.

4 – Uncertain Waits are Longer than Known, Finite Waits

Waiting seems to take longer when we don't know how long we are going to be waiting for. To overcome this, experience designers should seek to inform customers/clients or employees/staffs of how long they can expect to be waiting. There are many examples of this in practice in many different industries. One that most people are familiar with is the use of digital "downloading" bars that show how much longer it will take or a computer to finish downloading something. By providing users with this information, digital experience designers reduce the sense of waiting that customers/clients experience.

5 – Unexplained Waits are Longer than Explained Waits

The fifth Principles of Waiting is that our waits seem to last longer when we don't know why we are waiting. Given this, experience designers try to ensure that their customers/clients are kept informed of not only the duration of their expects waits, but also the reasons for these waits. For example, if an airplane is delayed in taking off, the captain will inform the passengers of both the expected duration of the delay and the reason for the delay.

6 – Unfair Waits are Longer than Equitable Waits

When people who are waiting feel that others are receiving faster service than they are, they are more acutely aware of the duration of their own waits. To overcome this, experience designers should ensure that their waiting processes are equitable.

3. How does profiling disruptive customers/clients assist customer contact personnel in dealing with "customers/clients from hell'?

Ans- With the growth of the service economy, there are high expectations on boundary-spanners to maintain customer satisfaction. However, the customers/clients today start to learn more tricks or principles of marketing. The company policies and marketing campaigns may become more vulnerable if they are flawed and consumers take advantage of them. Customers/clients are often welcomed, however, there are also some customers/clients that are not. In some cases, consumers rather believe that only when they resort to aggressive behaviors, they can be thought important. The corresponding aggressive or disordered behaviors vary differently according to the situation or needs. In a diary study of part-time service workers carried out by Grandey in 2002, 43% of anger-inducing interpersonal events reported over a 2-week period were due to consumers. In this term paper, I planned to do a study on the behavior of a special category called "customers/clients from hell" (CFH). Philip Kotler, one of the most prestigious management guru, placed the topic, Customer Satisfaction, as the third chapter of his book, Marketing Management, revealing the importance of dealing with customers/clients' values and satisfaction is the central concept of modern marketing. In this term paper, we are not trying to debate the effectiveness of the consumer-centric marketing. Instead, we want to categorize unusual disorder of consumer behaviors and try to formulate the mechanism of these behaviors. In addition, we also want to find the internal and external for these behaviors and analyze if some of those behaviors can indeed be rationalized according to the values we have or ethics we refer today

4. Why is the management of consumer waits and customer participation particularly important for service firms?

Ans- Customer participation is an important component of the service production process. If service providers can appropriately manage the participation, it will benefit both the companies and customers/clients. Otherwise, it will adversely affect the service outcomes. Through literature review, this article aims to provide guidelines regarding how to manage customer participation effectively. It covers definitions, benefits and drawbacks, as well as levels of customer participation. The difference between voluntary and involuntary participation will also be reviewed.

CONCLUSION

- This additional book under <u>MBA Basics in 24 Hours</u> helps you to get quick knowledge of Service Marketing and Management questions and answers.
- Short, simple summary & keywords can be used to present the whole topic in just less than three hours.
- The ideas and definitions can be used for examinations, viva and also knowledge sharing/transfer.
- Group discussions can be arranged and the above chapters are really helpful to bring out the best member in management.
- Examination papers can be set at the required levels in simple terms.
- The given information in all the chapters can also be used in schools, colleges and any other levels.
- Other eight books under 'MBA Basics in 24 hours' are also given in the same way to help out best for students and tutors (published in Amazon).

- Principles & Practices of Management
- Human Resource Management
- Financial Management
- Marketing Management
- Organisational Behaviour
- Managerial Economics
- Strategic Management
- Management Information Systems

For any feedback, query or suggestions please mail to astronara@gmail.com or info@zodiacservices.net.

You can also contact via www.zodiacservices.org/contact.

THANK YOU!